"ALL THAT IS WORTH CHERISHING BEGINS IN THE HEART..."

SUZANNE CHAPIN

Letters to You

Dear .... ,

THIS BOOK IS A CELEBRATION OF YOU. YOUR BRIGHT DREAMS,
YOUR UNIQUE TALENTS, YOUR FUNNIEST STORIES. IT'S ALSO A
BOOK ABOUT US. OUR ADVENTURES, OUR SECRET MOMENTS, OUR
GROWING UP TOGETHER. FROM YOUR FIRST BREATH, I KNEW YOU
WOULD CHANGE MY WORLD FOR THE BETTER, AND I'VE BEEN
FASCINATED WATCHING YOU CREATE YOUR OWN SPECIAL PLACE
IN THIS WORLD, DISCOVERING WHO YOU ARE, AND LEARNING
ALL THAT YOU ARE CAPABLE OF. MAY YOU FIND THESE REFLECTIONS
AND MEMORIES AS CHERISHED AS YOU ARE TO ME.

Love, ...

YOUR FIRST YEAR

1

WHEN I LOOK AT YOU, I SEE...

THESE DAYS, YOU REALLY LOVE...

I NEVER THOUGHT A YEAR AGO THAT YOU'D...

ONE THING I'LL ALWAYS REMEMBER
ABOUT THIS YEAR WITH YOU...

NO MATTER HOW OLD YOU ARE, I WILL ALWAYS PICTURE YOU...

My letter to you...

YOUR SECOND YEAR

2

MY BIGGEST DREAM FOR YOU IS...

YOU LAUGH EVERY TIME THAT...

I WAS SO EXCITED WHEN YOU STARTED TO...

ONE THING I'LL ALWAYS REMEMBER
ABOUT THIS YEAR WITH YOU...

SOME THINGS WE DO TOGETHER BEFORE YOU FALL ASLEEP ARE...

My letter to you...

YOUR THIRD YEAR

3

SOME SILLY THINGS YOU'VE SAID WERE...

SOME OF YOUR GREATEST ACCOMPLISHMENTS THIS YEAR WERE...

WHEN I SEE YOU SLEEPING, I FEEL...

ONE THING I'LL ALWAYS REMEMBER
ABOUT THIS YEAR WITH YOU...

SOME OF THE GIFTS YOU'VE GIVEN ME WERE...

"LOVE ONLY GROWS BY SHARING. YOU CAN ONLY HAVE MORE FOR YOURSELF BY GIVING IT AWAY TO OTHERS."

BRIAN TRACY

My letter to you...

YOUR FOURTH YEAR

4

YOUR FAVORITE GAME TO PLAY IS...

SOME OF OUR FAVORITE ACTIVITIES TO DO TOGETHER ARE...

YOU REALLY LIKE TO IMAGINE THAT...

ONE THING I'LL ALWAYS REMEMBER
ABOUT THIS YEAR WITH YOU...

I LOVE TO HEAR YOU...

My letter to you...

YOUR FIFTH YEAR

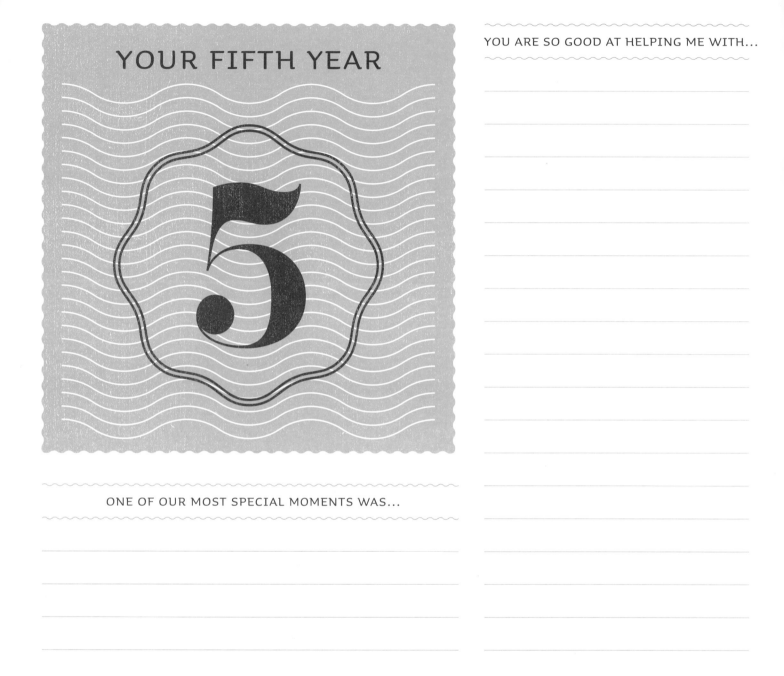

ONE OF OUR MOST SPECIAL MOMENTS WAS...

YOU ARE SO GOOD AT HELPING ME WITH...

YOU WERE REALLY BRAVE WHEN...

_____

_____

_____

_____

_____

_____

_____

ONE OF YOUR BEST FRIENDS IS:

_____

TOGETHER, YOU LIKE TO...

. . . .

. . . .

. . . .

. . . .

ONE THING I'LL ALWAYS REMEMBER
ABOUT THIS YEAR WITH YOU...

_____

_____

_____

_____

_____

_____

_____

_____

_____

_____

_____

_____

_____

_____

_____

_____

My letter to you...

You came into my life a brand new person, and yet, I've known you forever. Now that you are here, you've filled a space in my heart that I didn't know was missing. You are, and will always be, a dream fulfilled.

5¢

YOUR SIXTH YEAR

6

IF YOU COULD DO JUST ONE THING
ALL DAY, YOU WOULD...

MY HEART FILLS WITH JOY EVERY TIME YOU...

THE GRANDEST ADVENTURE WE WENT ON WAS...

ONE THING I'LL ALWAYS REMEMBER ABOUT THIS YEAR WITH YOU...

I WAS SO PROUD OF YOU WHEN...

*My letter
to you…*

YOUR SEVENTH YEAR

YOU ARE REALLY GOOD AT…

THE BEST STORY YOU TOLD WAS…

YOUR GREATEST DREAM IS...

ONE THING I'LL ALWAYS REMEMBER
ABOUT THIS YEAR WITH YOU...

MY BIGGEST WISH FOR YOU IS...

My letter to you...

YOUR EIGHTH YEAR

8

SOME THINGS YOU CAN'T GET ENOUGH OF ARE...

YOUR FAVORITE PLACE TO BE IS...

SOME IMPORTANT PEOPLE IN YOUR LIFE RIGHT NOW ARE...

ONE THING I'LL ALWAYS REMEMBER
ABOUT THIS YEAR WITH YOU...

I'M LOOKING FORWARD TO

WITH YOU BECAUSE...

My letter to you...

YOUR NINTH YEAR

9

ONE STRUGGLE YOU HAVE OVERCOME IS...

YOU ARE STARTING TO SHOW HOW GROWN UP YOU ARE BY...

ONE THING THAT ALWAYS COMES EASILY TO YOU IS...

ONE THING I'LL ALWAYS REMEMBER
ABOUT THIS YEAR WITH YOU...

YOU AMAZE ME WHEN YOU...

My letter to you...

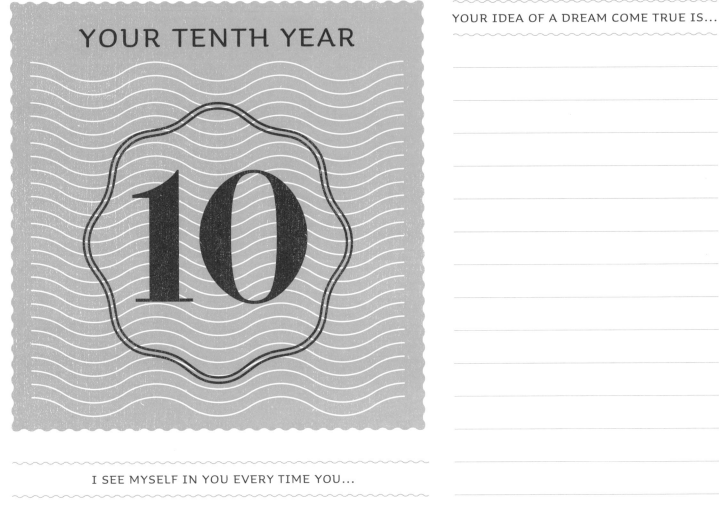

YOUR TENTH YEAR

10

I SEE MYSELF IN YOU EVERY TIME YOU...

YOUR IDEA OF A DREAM COME TRUE IS...

ONE DAY, I KNOW THAT YOU ARE GOING TO BE A GREAT...

ONE THING I'LL ALWAYS REMEMBER
ABOUT THIS YEAR WITH YOU...

YOUR FRIEND

IS VERY IMPORTANT TO YOU BECAUSE...

My letter to you...

There are moments with you when the world stands still, and we are the only ones in it—when everything falls away except our delight in each other. And for that moment, it's just you and me, celebrating us.

YOUR ELEVENTH YEAR

11

YOU ARE STARTING TO REALLY SHOW YOUR INDIVIDUALITY BY...

YOU CAN SPEND HOURS...

ONE IMPORTANT LESSON YOU'VE LEARNED THIS YEAR IS...

ONE THING I'LL ALWAYS REMEMBER
ABOUT THIS YEAR WITH YOU...

NO MATTER HOW OLD YOU ARE, I WILL ALWAYS PICTURE YOU...

My letter to you...

YOUR TWELFTH YEAR

12

ONE OF THE MOST MEANINGFUL THINGS
YOU DID THIS YEAR WAS...

IT AMAZES ME HOW
TALENTED YOU ARE AT...

YOU SHOW YOUR LOVE FOR YOUR FAMILY BY...

ONE THING I'LL ALWAYS REMEMBER
ABOUT THIS YEAR WITH YOU...

A SPECIAL WAY THAT WE CONNECT IS...

My letter to you...

YOUR THIRTEENTH YEAR

13

SOME WAYS THAT YOU'VE
GROWN UP IN THE LAST YEAR...

I COULD NEVER HAVE IMAGINED THAT
ONE DAY YOU'D BE ABLE TO...

ONE WAY I SEE MYSELF IN YOU IS...

ONE THING I'LL ALWAYS REMEMBER ABOUT THIS YEAR WITH YOU...

ONE WAY YOU ARE COMPLETELY UNIQUE IS...

> "LOVE IS TO LOVE SOMEONE FOR
> WHO THEY ARE, WHO THEY WERE,
> AND WHO THEY WILL BE."
> CHRIS MOORE

My letter to you...

YOUR FOURTEENTH YEAR

14

YOU ARE BECOMING AN AMAZING YOUNG ADULT BY...

ONE WAY YOU'VE SHOWN JUST HOW COURAGEOUS YOU ARE IS...

OUR BEST CONVERSATIONS HAVE BEEN ABOUT...

ONE THING I'LL ALWAYS REMEMBER
ABOUT THIS YEAR WITH YOU...

SOME THINGS YOU ARE REALLY GIFTED AT ARE...

My letter to you...

YOUR FIFTEENTH YEAR

15

YOU IMPRESS ME WITH THE WAY YOU...

AN IMPORTANT DECISION YOU'VE MADE ON YOUR OWN IS...

TIMES THAT YOU'VE STAYED TRUE TO WHO YOU ARE...

ONE THING I'LL ALWAYS REMEMBER
ABOUT THIS YEAR WITH YOU...

TIMES THAT WE'VE LAUGHED THE HARDEST WERE...

My letter to you...

You are your own person. You are shaping

a new path, a new way, a new story.

You are a gift the world has not seen before.

You are like no other.

YOUR SIXTEENTH YEAR

16

SOME WAYS THAT YOU HAVE ASSERTED
YOUR INDEPENDENCE ARE...

IT'S WONDERFUL TO WATCH YOU...

I'VE NEVER BEEN PROUDER OF YOU THAN WHEN...

ONE THING I'LL ALWAYS REMEMBER
ABOUT THIS YEAR WITH YOU...

THE MOST IMPORTANT PERSON
IN YOUR LIFE RIGHT NOW IS

BECAUSE...

My letter to you…

YOUR SEVENTEENTH YEAR

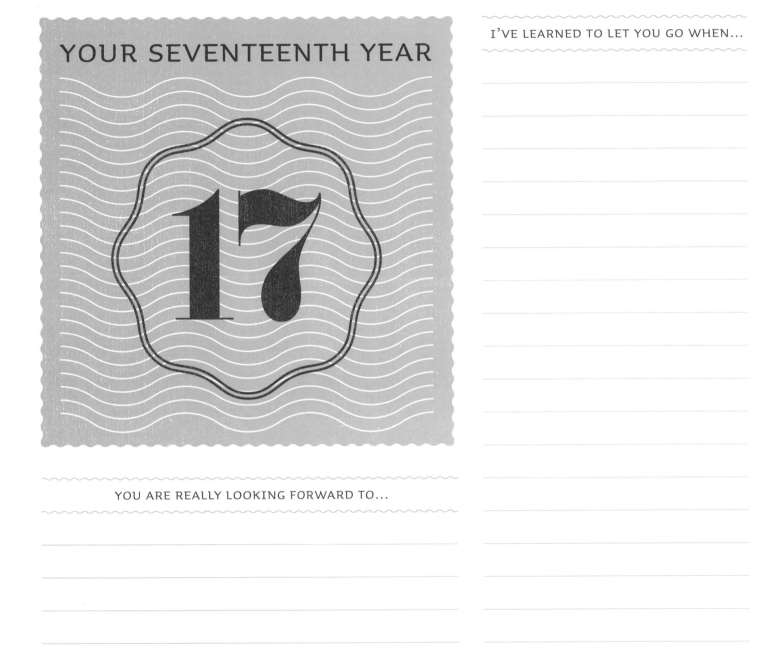

I'VE LEARNED TO LET YOU GO WHEN...

YOU ARE REALLY LOOKING FORWARD TO...

A TIME YOU SURPRISED ME WAS WHEN...

ONE THING I'LL ALWAYS REMEMBER
ABOUT THIS YEAR WITH YOU...

SOMEONE YOU LOOK UP TO IS

BECAUSE...

*My letter
to you...*

YOUR EIGHTEENTH YEAR

18

THROUGH THE YEARS, IT'S BEEN THRILLING TO SEE YOU...

A GOAL YOU WERE PROUD
OF REACHING WAS...

YOU'VE TAUGHT ME...

ONE THING I'LL ALWAYS REMEMBER
ABOUT THIS YEAR WITH YOU...

I ADMIRE HOW YOU...

My letter to you...

COMPENDIUM®
live inspired

....

WRITTEN BY: MIRIAM HATHAWAY
DESIGNED BY: HEIDI RODRIGUEZ
EDITED BY: AMELIA RIEDLER AND M.H. CLARK
CREATIVE DIRECTION BY: JULIE FLAHIFF

....

WITH LOVE FOR MY MOTHER, WHO HAS TAKEN ME ON SOME WILD AND WONDERFUL ADVENTURES. AND RIVER AND WILL, WHO ARE TAKING ME ON MY GRANDEST ADVENTURE YET.
Miriam

ISBN: 978-1-938298-57-8

9th printing. Printed in China with soy inks.

Create meaningful moments with gifts that inspire.

CONNECT WITH US
live-inspired.com | sayhello@compendiuminc.com

   @compendiumliveinspired
#compendiumliveinspired